FRANCIS FRITH'S

ACCRINGTON OLD
PHOTOGRAPHIC Memories

THE FRANCIS FRITH COLLECTION

www.francisfrith.com

FRANCIS FRITH'S

ACCRINGTON
OLD AND NEW

PHOTOGRAPHIC MEMORIES

HELEN BARRETT considers herself an Accringtonian, having lived here for over 45 years. Both she and **CATHERINE DUCKWORTH** are graduate chartered librarians, and have job-shared the post of Local Studies Librarian at Accrington Library since 1992. They are both members of the Hyndburn Local History Society.

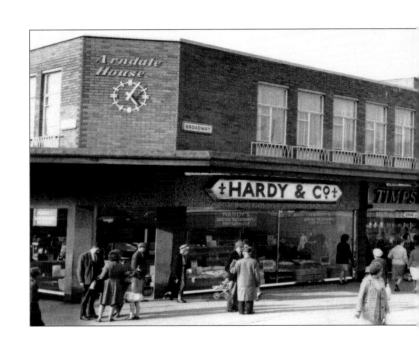

FRANCIS FRITH'S
PHOTOGRAPHIC MEMORIES

ACCRINGTON
OLD AND NEW

PHOTOGRAPHIC MEMORIES

HELEN BARRETT AND
CATHERINE DUCKWORTH

First published in the United Kingdom in 2004 by
Frith Book Company Ltd

Limited Hardback Subscribers Edition Published in 2004
ISBN 1-85937-805-6

Paperback Edition 2004
ISBN 1-85937-806-4

British Library Cataloguing in Publication Data

Francis Frith's Accrington Old and New - Photographic Memories
Helen Barrett and Catherine Duckworth

Frith Book Company Ltd
Frith's Barn, Teffont,
Salisbury, Wiltshire SP3 5QP
Tel: +44 (0) 1722 716 376
Email: info@francisfrith.co.uk
www.francisfrith.co.uk

Printed and bound in Great Britain

Front Cover: **ACCRINGTON**, *Blackburn Road 1899* 43496t
Frontispiece: **ACCRINGTON**, *Broadway c1965* A19024

Additional (2004) photographs by Helen Barrett and Catherine Duckworth

*The colour-tinting is for illustrative purposes only, and is
not intended to be historically accurate*

CONTENTS

FRANCIS FRITH
VICTORIAN PIONEER

FRANCIS FRITH, founder of the world-famous photographic archive, was a complex and multi-talented man. A devout Quaker and a highly successful Victorian businessman, he was philosophical by nature and pioneering in outlook.

By 1855 he had already established a wholesale grocery business in Liverpool, and sold it for the astonishing sum of £200,000, which is the equivalent today of over £15,000,000. Now a very rich man, he was able to indulge his passion for travel. As a child he had pored over travel books written by early explorers, and his fancy and imagination had been stirred by family holidays to the sublime mountain regions of Wales and Scotland. 'What lands of spirit-stirring and enriching scenes and places!' he had written. He was to return to these scenes of grandeur in later years to 'recapture the thousands of vivid and tender memories', but with a different purpose. Now in his thirties, and captivated by the new science of photography, Frith set out on a series of

pioneering journeys up the Nile and to the Near East that occupied him from 1856 until 1860.

INTRIGUE AND EXPLORATION

These far-flung journeys were packed with intrigue and adventure. In his life story, written when he was sixty-three, Frith tells of being held captive by bandits, and of fighting 'an awful midnight battle to the very point of surrender with a deadly pack of hungry, wild dogs'. Wearing flowing Arab costume, Frith arrived at Akaba by camel sixty years before Lawrence of Arabia, where he encountered 'desert princes and rival sheikhs, blazing with jewel-hilted swords'.

He was the first photographer to venture beyond the sixth cataract of the Nile. Africa was still the mysterious 'Dark Continent', and Stanley and Livingstone's historic meeting was a decade into the future. The conditions for picture taking confound belief. He laboured for hours in his wicker dark-room in the sweltering heat of the desert, while the volatile chemicals fizzed dangerously in their trays. Back in London he exhibited his photographs and was 'rapturously cheered' by members of the Royal Society. His reputation as a photographer was made overnight.

VENTURE OF A LIFE-TIME

Characteristically, Frith quickly spotted the opportunity to create a new business as a specialist publisher of photographs. He lived in an era of immense and sometimes violent change. For the poor in the early part of Victoria's

reign work was exhausting and the hours long, and people had precious little free time to enjoy themselves. Most had no transport other than a cart or gig at their disposal, and rarely travelled far beyond the boundaries of their own town or village. However, by the 1870s the railways had threaded their way across the country, and Bank Holidays and half-day Saturdays had been made obligatory by Act of Parliament. All of a sudden the working man and his family were able to enjoy days out and see a little more of the world.

With typical business acumen, Francis Frith foresaw that these new tourists would enjoy having souvenirs to commemorate their days out. In 1860 he married Mary Ann Rosling and set out on a new career: his aim was to photograph every city, town and village in Britain. For the next thirty years he travelled the country by train and by pony and trap, producing fine photographs of seaside resorts and beauty spots that were keenly bought by millions of Victorians. These prints were painstakingly pasted into family albums and pored over during the dark nights of winter, rekindling precious memories of summer excursions.

THE RISE OF FRITH & CO

Frith's studio was soon supplying retail shops all over the country. To meet the demand he gathered about him a small team of photographers, and published the work of independent artist-photographers of the calibre of Roger Fenton and Francis Bedford. In order to gain some understanding of the scale of Frith's business one only has to look at the catalogue issued by Frith & Co in 1886: it runs to some 670 pages, listing not only many thousands of views of the British Isles but also many photographs of most European countries, and China, Japan, the USA and Canada - note the sample page shown on page 9 from the hand-written Frith & Co ledgers recording the pictures. By 1890 Frith had created the greatest specialist photographic publishing company in the world, with over 2,000 sales outlets - more than the combined number that Boots and WH Smith have today! The picture on the next page shows the Frith & Co display board at Ingleton in the Yorkshire Dales (left of window). Beautifully constructed with a mahogany frame and gilt inserts, it could display up to a dozen local scenes.

POSTCARD BONANZA

The ever-popular holiday postcard we know today took many years to develop. In 1870 the Post Office issued the first plain cards, with a pre-printed stamp on one face. In 1894 they allowed other publishers' cards to be sent through the mail with an attached adhesive halfpenny stamp. Demand grew rapidly, and in 1895 a new size of postcard was permitted called the court card, but there was little room for illustration. In 1899, a year after Frith's death, a new card measuring 5.5 x 3.5 inches became the standard format, but it was not until 1902 that the divided back came into being, so that the address and message could be on one face and a full-size illustration on the other. Frith & Co were in the vanguard of postcard development: Frith's sons Eustace and Cyril continued their father's monumental task, expanding the number of views offered to the public and recording more and more places in Britain, as the coasts and countryside were opened up to mass travel.

Francis Frith had died in 1898 at his villa in Cannes, his great project still growing. The archive he created continued in business for another seventy years. By 1970 it contained over a third of a million pictures showing 7,000 British towns and villages.

FRANCIS FRITH'S LEGACY

Frith's legacy to us today is of immense significance and value, for the magnificent archive of evocative photographs he created provides a unique record of change in the cities, towns and villages throughout Britain over a century and more. Frith and his fellow studio photographers revisited locations many times down the years to update their views, compiling for us an enthralling and colourful pageant of British life and character.

We are fortunate that Frith was dedicated to recording the minutiae of everyday life. For it is this sheer wealth of visual data, the painstaking chronicle of changes in dress, transport, street layouts, buildings, housing, engineering and landscape that captivates us so much today. His remarkable images offer us a powerful link with the past and with the lives of our ancestors.

THE VALUE OF THE ARCHIVE TODAY

Computers have now made it possible for Frith's many thousands of images to be accessed almost instantly. Frith's images are increasingly used as visual resources, by social historians, by researchers into genealogy and ancestry, by architects and town planners, and by teachers involved in local history projects.

In addition, the archive offers every one of us an opportunity to examine the places where we and our families have lived and worked down the years. Highly successful in Frith's own era, the archive is now, a century and more on, entering a new phase of popularity. Historians consider the Francis Frith Collection to be of prime national importance. It is the only archive of its kind remaining in private ownership. Francis Frith's archive is now housed in an historic timber barn in the beautiful village of Teffont in Wiltshire. Its founder would not recognize the archive office as it is today. In place of the many thousands of dusty boxes containing glass plate negatives and an all-pervading odour of photographic chemicals, there are now ranks of computer screens. He would be amazed to watch his images travelling round the world at unimaginable speeds through internet lines.

The archive's future is both bright and exciting. Francis Frith, with his unshakeable belief in making photographs available to the greatest number of people, would undoubtedly approve of what is being done today with his lifetime's work. His photographs depicting our shared past are now bringing pleasure and enlightenment to millions around the world a century and more after his death.

ACCRINGTON
OLD AND NEW

AN INTRODUCTION

MENTION Accrington to most people and they immediately think of Accrington Stanley, that most famous of all football teams. How sad that there are no photographs of Accrington Stanley in the Frith archive, nor of the Accrington Pals, the famous locally raised First World War regiment who suffered such severe casualties. The photographers employed by Francis Frith tended to portray the town centre, the churches, important buildings, social and cultural institutions and places of recreation. This is certainly true of the collection of photographs relating to Accrington and district. We have cause to be thankful to these photographers who so faithfully recorded the development and changes in our town.

The name Accrington is of Saxon origin. However, the earliest tangible evidence of a settlement at Accrington is a charter of circa 1140, in which Henry de Lacy granted Elvethem (Altham) and Akerington (Accrington) to Hugh, son of Leofwine. About 1200, Accrington was detached and given to the abbot and monks of Kirkstall by Robert de Lacy. Later in the 16th century there were local disturbances over the enclosure of wasteland. During the Civil War,

two local Parliamentarians, Nicholas Cunliffe of Hollins and Robert Cunliffe of Sparth, played prominent parts against the Royalists in Lancashire.

During the 17th and 18th centuries, the staple industries of the area were the spinning and weaving of woollen cloth, and Accrington and district's development really began towards the end of the 18th century. Factories were built from 1760; the first was Brookside Printworks in Oswaldtwistle, where Robert Peel installed the first spinning jennies invented by James Hargreaves. Another local man, John Hacking of Huncoat, invented the first carding engine in 1772. It was turned by hand, and was used for cleaning and straightening the cotton before spinning - Hacking carded cotton wool for his neighbours. By 1774, the demand for cotton goods had increased so much that the manufacture of pure cotton was legalised. A record of 1780 states that in Accrington there were five small spinning mills employing forty people. This was the beginning of the factory system. A survey of New Accrington in 1790 recorded three carding engines; two dyehouses; one fulling mill; one loom house; and one pencilling shop. Broad Oak Printworks were established in 1792 in a steep valley; the works relied on the mountain stream for its waterpower. This centre of industry brought about a major increase in the population of the town as houses began to be built in the area close by. By 1801 the population was 3,077.

Steam power was introduced in 1816, and by 1818 calico printing was losing ground to the cotton spinning and weaving industry; the woollen trade was virtually extinct. By 1823 power looms were beginning to replace handlooms, and in May 1826 between 3,000 and 4,000 handloom weavers, fearing for the loss of their livelihood, attacked Grange Mill during the power loom riots. The cotton industry expanded at such a pace that seventeen weaving sheds and mills were built in the ten-year period beginning in 1850. The industry was thriving. Accrington concentrated on the production of coarse cotton cloth, such as 'dhooties', and the majority of it was exported. Much of it went to India.

The cotton famine in America was a temporary setback to the growth of the cotton industry. By 1884 there were 27,011 looms installed, and by 1910 the figure was 36,100. The early years of the 20th century were the golden days for the cotton industry. In 1911 there were thirty-eight cotton mills in Accrington, and the census returns showed that 41.5% of the working population was employed in the cotton industry. The population had then peaked at 45,029.

The decline of the cotton trade began soon after the First World War. It was a gradual process as some of the countries who had been the Lancashire cotton industry's best customers began to develop their own industry. Frequently, Howard & Bullough's supplied the spinning and weaving machinery to allow countries to do this. The whole industry went into decline, with the weaving industry being especially hard hit. After 1929, redundant machinery was scrapped at an alarming rate. Many mills stood 'silent' - not working, but still filled with machinery. The mills with a full order book were fortunate, but the failure to re-equip with new machinery and to reorganise meant that many mills had to diversify and change the type of cloth they manufactured. At the time of the 1931 census, there were 3,843 out of work in Accrington.

The preparations for war meant a change in the situation, and a labour surplus was changed into a labour shortage. In 1941 Terylene, later known as Polyester, was invented by a team of scientists led by Whinfield and Dixon working at Broad Oak. Their discovery was to have far-reaching ramifications. The post-war boom in the cotton industry lasted until the early 1950s, when short-time working and temporary closures of mills once more became more frequent. By 1958 competition from abroad, especially from Asian countries in the Commonwealth, was so intense that more cotton cloth was imported than exported. In 1959 the cotton industry was reorganised under a government scheme, and by 1960 only a third of the looms and spindles that had been in the town in 1931 remained.

As industries evolved in the 19th century, better communications became necessary, and so the turnpike roads began to be built. The first of these was the Whalley to Abbey Street, built by John Metcalf in 1790. The Blackburn and Burnley roads followed in 1826-27 and 1838 respectively. The Leeds to Liverpool canal, which had begun in 1799, was cut between Burnley and Clayton-le-Moors in 1816. Some means of transport was necessary for moving the manufactured goods and coal, and the East Lancashire Railway was extended from Bury in 1848. The railway age had begun, and Accrington Station opened in 1848. The Accrington railway viaduct, a monumental piece of Victorian engineering and described as Accrington's finest structure, was erected in 1847 and restored in 1866. By 1849 there were three railway lines, to Blackburn, Burnley and Manchester. Steam trams made their first appearance in the town in 1886, with services running from the Market Place to Clayton, Church and Baxenden. Shortly afterwards the service was extended to Haslingden. Many people found the steam trams noisy and uncomfortable, but the opportunity they offered to travel around the area made them very popular. Electric trams replaced steam in 1907, and new routes were added. A bus service began in 1922, and the first Corporation buses ran in November 1929. The first services ran from the Market Place to Huncoat Station, and to Higher Antley and Woodnook.

The raw materials and natural resources of the area were shale, stone and coal, and there is evidence of mining from the 18th century at Laund, Green Haworth and Moleside Moor. Organised mining began in the early 19th century, and the industry soon occupied a key position in the economy of the area. There were several collieries; some, like Scaitcliffe, sunk in 1860, were surprisingly close to the town centre. Warmden Quarry was worked and provided building stone, setts and kerbs.

Several important events in Accrington's history occurred in the mid 19th century. In 1840 the police force appeared, and the following year the Accrington Gas and Water Company came

into being. In 1853 the Local Board of Health was formed and the 1848 Public Health Act was adopted. The Local Board began to clean up the town - without any control before this, poor living standards had become the norm. The Board of Health Inquiry of 1851 had shown that there were 1,653 houses for a population of 10,000; of these, 124 consisted of a single room. There were numerous open drains and cesspits close to the houses; 778 houses were without an individual water supply, and many had wells in their cellars. Most of the inhabitants fetched their water from the nearest public well or spring, of which there were several in the town. It was not until 1889 that an adequate sewerage system was provided. But the Board of Health was also active on the building front. The Peel Institution, later the Town Hall, was erected by public subscription in 1854, and in 1869 the Market Hall was erected at a cost of £6,500 and opened amidst joyful celebrations. This same building still stands - a monument to the foresight of the members of the Local Board. The clock, protected by cherubs and fruit, has been working hard since 1869. The Local Board was also responsible for providing the cemetery on Burnley Road; the first burial took place in 1864.

In 1853 the Globe Works of Howard & Bleakley (later Howard & Bullough) were established, and marked the beginning of Accrington's engineering industry. The manufacture of textile machinery, printing machinery and in particular the Rabbeth spindle in the town gave Accrington tremendous prestige, as its products began to be exported worldwide. Globe Works became the biggest industrial undertaking in Accrington. Coupled with the advancing cotton industry,

Accrington was developing as a factory town. Relatively high wages attracted workers from the outlying areas, and by 1861 the population was over 17,000. In 1857 Lang Bridge founded Paradise Street Works, making iron and tinplate products, including iron bedsteads and kitchen ranges. Dowry Works, established by Christopher and Thomas Whittaker, produced brick-making machinery. The Ewbank carpet sweeper was manufactured by Entwistle & Kenyon from 1889. The famous Blake's hydraulic ram was made at Oxford Street Works by John Blake. Over four thousand people were employed in engineering in Accrington in 1911.

The life of the Local Board came to an end in 1878 when Accrington was incorporated as a Borough, adopting the motto 'Industry and Prudence Conquer'. The townspeople elected their first councillors, and judging from the election material preserved in Accrington Local Studies Library, it was an election worth witnessing. The first meeting of the council was held on 9 May 1878, and Alderman John Emmanuel Lightfoot was elected as Mayor. His portrait is still displayed on the landing in Accrington Library. The Peel Institution became the Town Hall, and the first Town Clerk was Edmund Whittaker.

Union Street, the first planned street in Accrington, was constructed in 1787. At this time Accrington was still a growing village, clustered around St James' church, Bull Bridge and Abbey Street; now separate communities began to be established, each developing its own identity. Each community centred round its mill, its church, its chapel, its shops and its school. Building bylaws were introduced by the Corporation as whole streets of terraced houses appeared, laid out in a gridiron pattern and unaffected by the contours of the land. The mill would be situated close to a water supply, and the workers' housing clustered around the mill.

There was plenty for Accringtonians to do in their spare time; most of the churches and chapels had men's institutes, women's groups, and choirs, and amateur dramatic societies thrived. The Accrington Naturalists' Society (later known as the Accrington Naturalists' and Antiquarians' Society) was established in 1855. The swimming baths opened in 1879 on the initiative of Eli Higham. The first evidence of live theatre in Accrington is a poster from 1860 advertising the Theatre Royal at the Peel Institution. The Hippodrome Theatre on Ellison Street opened in 1903, burnt down in 1908, and then reopened six months later with seating accommodation for 1,600. The Dowry Street Picture Palace, opened in 1910, was reputed to be the first permanent cinema in Accrington. In the next twelve years, no less than four cinemas opened - the King's Hall, the Empire, the Palace and the Ritz. The Regal, later renamed the Odeon, opened in 1937.

The town centre, with its regular market and high-class individual shops, attracted shoppers from the outlying districts and the neighbouring towns. Visitors flocked to the parks, the art gallery and the museum. So shall we go and look round the town and see what the photographers from Francis Frith & Company found so interesting?

BLACKBURN ROAD

THE main route and former turnpike through to Blackburn has always been a main shopping street. Until recent changes to the road system created a mini-roundabout at the junction with St James' Street and Broadway and a pedestrianised zone outside the Town Hall, it was always a busy, bustling thoroughfare. The shops are no longer all the fashionable shops of Accrington's former glory days, but the Town Hall and Market Hall still remain the imposing buildings they always were and form a valuable centrepiece to town life.

The Town Hall was built to commemorate Sir Robert Peel, whose family have long connections with the area; it was opened in 1858. The Market Hall was opened in 1869, and is one of the few Victorian market buildings in the country still in use for its original purpose. It is a testament to the foresight of the Local Board of Health, who planned and developed the site. It was built of local stone and is richly ornamented. Despite its considerable size, it soon proved to be insufficient, and for many years temporary stalls were erected outside each market day. The concrete 'umbrella' market was built in 1962 and was soon in regular use, until it was cleared to make way for the new market and shops that opened in 2003.

Greetings from Accrington, Composite c1955 A19018

The views are of the Town Hall in the centre, the sunken gardens on Broadway, the Parkinson Rock Garden in Oak Hill Park, Blackburn Road and St James' Church. Many an exiled Accringtonian would have been happy to receive this reminder of his or her home town.

Blackburn Road c1915
A19004

This part of Blackburn Road was a hive of activity with lots of shops. The electric tram (just visible under the bridge) shows that the photograph was taken after 1907, when the old steam trams of the Baltic Fleet were withdrawn. The Baptist chapel (centre left) was built in 1836, but since a larger building was erected on Cannon Street in 1874, it has undergone many changes of use.

◀ *Blackburn Road c1955* A19015

In a few yards there were many clothes shops here, including Weaver to Wearer, Burtons and Fifty Shilling Tailors Ltd. The building on the corner of Broadway with the stylish curved frontage (right) housed Woods the tobacconist's and Porter's Wallpapers, both familiar names to Accringtonians over many years.

▲ *Blackburn Road 2004* A19701

Once this was the part of the street with clothing shops; it is now the part of town with the banks, building societies and estate agents. The accommodation in the upper floors, no longer needed for shop storage, is available for offices. The cast iron lampposts show a return to Victorian styles, with the hanging baskets a brave attempt to cheer up the area.

◄ *The Town Hall c1965* A19025

This busy junction had cars battling for right of way. On the opposite corner from the Yorkshire Bank was Redman's the grocer's (centre right), beloved by local housewives for their selection and good value. Beyond that, the Co-op furniture store is in the building which was formerly the home of Woolworth's.

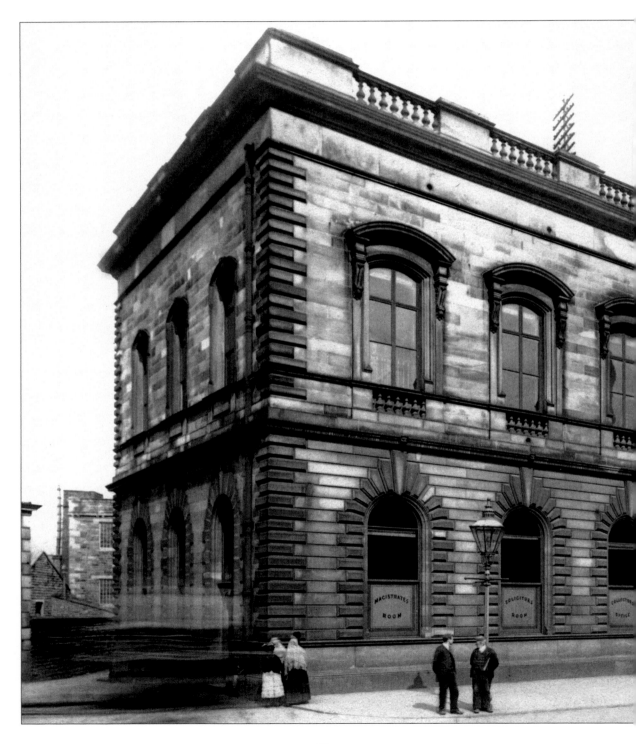

The Town Hall 1897
40119

The Town Hall was
originally known as the
Peel Institution, and
was used as Assembly
Rooms. The etching on
the windows, 'Magistrates
Room' and 'Solicitors
Room', reminds us that
the Magistrates' Courts
were also housed here
for many years. The
police station, just visible
behind on the left at
the top of Union Street,
was accessible from the
court via an underground
passage for the prisoners
to pass through on their
way from dock to cell. The
imposing ballroom has
seen many gatherings of
different types, including
the Grand Fancy Dress
Ball that is advertised on
the large poster along
with the Cyclists Parade.
These events were amongst
fundraising activities
for the provision of a
Cottage Hospital. Recently
refurbished, the ballroom is
still in regular use today for
a variety of events.

▼ *The Town Hall c1910* A19002

The handsome portico of the building has been the position from which civic dignitaries have overseen events such as the march past of the Accrington Pals on their way to training in August 1915. The poster advertises houses for sale: this was the time when the town was experiencing its greatest growth.

▶ *The Town Hall 2004*
A19702

Blackburn Road has been pedestrianised, enabling improved street furniture and planting. Its stonework now clean and smart, the Town Hall in 2004 still holds the Council Chamber, and also houses the Tourist Information Centre. Visitors walk onto the original Italian mosaic floor that was recently carefully restored.

◀ *The Town Hall*
1897 40118

Land behind the Town Hall was used for industry for many years: the Spring Mill buildings and the cupola of Pleck Brass Works are visible to the right. Notice also the stonework at the back of the Town Hall in front of the mill so that a future extension could be keyed in. The pub on the left of the photo was the Thwaites Arms, demolished to make way for Broadway.

▶ *The Town Hall*
c1955 A19014

The Town Hall is showing the grime of the passing years. The bus shelter rather spoiling its frontage was for those people waiting to go to Haslingden and Bacup. The old Fish Market is just visible on the right, with the Odeon showing behind.

► *The Town Hall*
c1965 A19030

An elegant lamp standard adorns the zebra crossing in front of the Town Hall, and hanging baskets brighten the stonework. The shops on the right are on the site of the Piccadilly shops built by Edmund Hepple using the compensation for loss of use of his corn mill during the building of the railway viaduct.

◄ *The Market Hall*
c1965 A19026

The area at the front of the Market Hall became a favourite meeting place with its wide pavement, seats and sunny aspect. Proximity to the bus station kept this area busy. There was still plenty of on-street parking at this time, before Accrington developed various car parks. It is still striving to keep parking free.

▲ *The Market Hall 1897* 40117

The Market Hall was designed to complement the adjacent Town Hall, and it is a massive structure. It has always housed many stalls selling a wide assortment of goods.

◄ *The Market Hall c1965*
A19021

The outside stalls made way for flower planters and trees, and neat railings direct foot traffic to safer road crossings. The Central Bus Terminus was completed at this date, and so were the new 'umbrella' markets behind the Market Hall.

Blackburn Road 1897
40116

Although not a market day, there is still plenty of activity along the road. Henry Wormwell, a mill and general furnishing engineer, had premises on the corner of Piccadilly, the block of shops just opposite the Town Hall. The block opposite the Market Hall was demolished and rebuilt as more imposing shops in about 1924.

*The Market
2004* A19703

The new outside
market stalls
which stretch
along the Peel
Street side and
the back of the
Market Hall
were built in
2003 to replace
the concrete
umbrella market,
which was
demolished
in 2002. The
skylights of the
new building can
be seen to echo
those of the old.

The Market Hall 2004 A19704

The figures on top of the Market Hall were removed for five years when sewerage work was being undertaken nearby, but they were returned after cleaning and repair in December 1986. According to the reports of the opening of the building, they represent industry, commerce and agriculture. The cornucopia with cherubs on either side of the clock illustrates the produce available inside the building.

The Bus Station
c1965 A19020

The buses are bedecked in Accrington Corporation's distinctive dark blue and red livery. A narrow black line around the windows was added to commemorate the losses suffered by the Accrington Pals in the First World War. The 'Gordon' tram shelter had previously stood on Peel Street, and was demolished in 1953. After many delays the new bus station was constructed in 1963.

◄ *Detail from A19020*

◄ *Blackburn Road c1965* A19022

Garth Dawson's Camera Cabin, located behind the clock (centre, behind the bus), has had several locations around the centre of Accrington, and is now sited round the corner on Blackburn Road. E J Riley's, once the towering giant of snooker and billiards and based in the town, had a shop on the left. They also made other sports equipment such as golf clubs and bowls.

◄ The Bus Station and the New Market 2004 A19706

The main part of the new outside market lies along Peel Street; its construction forced the alteration of the bus station into a line of stands on each side of the street. The break in the middle allows the skylight of the central passageway of the new building to reflect the shape of the decoration on the Market Hall.

▲ The Market and the Bus Station 2004 A19705

Although Hyndburn Council has not owned any buses since 1996, a new bus station was provided by the Council alongside the market development in 2003. The building on the right is Peel Street Baptist Church, originally known as Ebenezer Baptist.

◄ Blackburn Road 2004 A19707

The main buildings are little changed in over one hundred years, and the awnings over the shops seem tidier; but the proliferation of signs is messier. In front of Ogden's the jeweller's (centre left), formerly Cash Clothing, is the clock erected to commemorate the Golden Jubilee of Queen Elizabeth II.

*Blackburn Road
1899* 43496

The Cash Clothing
building (left) later
became Lloyds
Bank. The boot
sign halfway up
the road on the
right is the Golden
Boot, the premises
of Fred Dugdale,
whose shop was
equipped with ' a
private fitting room
for ladies'. A sign
opposite exhorts us
to drink Altham's
2/4 tea; Altham's
started by selling
tea in 1864, and
then began taking
their customers on
trips. Thus began
a travel agency
which developed
branches over a
wide area, and
continues today.

31

▶ *Blackburn Road 2004* A19708

This view looks back towards the junction with Church Street and Peel Street again; the upper view of the buildings is little changed from earlier days. The imposing shop premises that were formerly those of J W Bridge, an ironmonger's, with the lead-roofed turret embellishing the corner, still looks attractive.

▼ *Blackburn Road c1955* A19013

We are looking down towards the Market and the Town Hall, with the Lloyds Bank building beyond the Savoy Café (right) - Lloyds Bank moved to Whalley Road in 1962. The road surface is still the traditional hardwearing setts, and the position of the former tramlines can be made out. Thornber's the chemist's, to be seen on the left under the 'H' sign, had branches throughout the area. The shop was later known as Espley's.

▶ *Blackburn Road 2004* A19709

As we come away from the main shopping centre, the buildings become less imposing and only two stories in height; but still the stone façades prevail. Just on the left along Bridge Street was a borehole testing for the coal seam, and it is not surprising that when the lift shaft was being dug for the Argos store on the higher corner that coal should be found only a few feet below the surface. This is indeed the edge of the Burnley Coalfield.

◄ *Blackburn Road 2004* A19710

The opposite side of the road from A19709 (above) shows the new frontage of Altham's, now very much a travel firm; the tea sales are a distant memory, although the shop still occupies the same site.

Broadway Gardens c1955
A19016

The Broadway sunken gardens were constructed in 1952 after the area had been the subject of controversy for some years. Derelict land on both sides of Broadway was screened by wooden hoardings, and there were many complaints about this barren and unsightly part of town. The plans were part of a post-war improvement scheme which originated in a town plan produced by Mattocks and Allen, two town planners with visionary ideas. It is sad that not many of their ideas for the rejuvenation of the town centre were ever put into place, mainly because the

finance was not available. The River Hyndburn, which flowed through this area, was culverted by the Borough Engineer's

Broadway c1965 A19023

We are looking into Broadway and Union Street towards the newly opened Arndale Centre. The doorway on the side of the Town Hall has now been made up into a window, with the new stone looking considerably cleaner than the original.

Broadway 2004
A19711

The main change visible here is in the road system, with a one-way system operating from Broadway and the road surface being mainly brick. The opportunity has been taken to plant trees to brighten the scene. The shops in Arndale House have changed over the years; they have gradually reduced in floor size and increased in numbers.

Broadway c1965 A19024

The Arndale House shops opened in September 1961. Whilst some of these shops were newcomers to the town - Hardy & Co the furnishers, Macfisheries, and Marks & Spencer - others relocated to Broadway from other parts of the town. Woolworth's later moved here next to Marks & Spencer.

▶ *Broadway
2004* A19712

The well-grown tree hides Arndale House and the new Cornhill development, but the ugly Town Hall extension of 1966 (right) is still in clear sight.

◀ *Broadway c1965* A19032

The hoardings on the right cover the work being done on the new extension to the Town Hall, which was to be completed in April 1966. The new Broadway and the shops proved immediately popular, and linked through with the outside market. The Coppice can be seen in the distance.

◄ *The Market c1965*
A19019

The new outside market was opened in October 1962. Its concrete 'umbrella' roof based on cylindrical sections allowed for fewer columns and greater flexibility of arrangement. Pleck Road through to Peel Street is just visible on the left of the photograph. The Market soon became popular, but it was demolished in 2002 to make way for new shops, and another new outside market was built on Peel Street.

◄ *Broadway
2004* A19713

The Arndale
House building
is much the
same, but
the cinema has
made way for
the Cornhill
shops, and
beyond the
canopy of
the Town Hall
extension are
the new shops
which have
replaced the
outside markets.
Broadway itself
shows the scars
from the flower
beds, which
were removed
so that the
temporary
market stalls
could be erected
here during the
building work.

▲ *The Market c1965* A19034

The neat fencing separating the market from Broadway was later removed to facilitate shoppers.
Higher up Broadway, on the right, was Catlow's the greengrocer's. The Odeon was also known as
the Regal and later Unit 4 – this was an odd name, as it only had three screens.

◄ *Broadway
2004* A19714

The new shops
on Broadway are
on the site of the
former outside
market. Also just
visible on the
left are the new
Cornhill shops,
which are on the
site of the Odeon
cinema.

THE PARKS

FEW towns the size of Accrington could boast as many public parks, nor, during the time that Frith's photographers were here, could other towns match the brilliant floral displays of bedding plants grown in the Corporation's own greenhouses.

The first park in the town was Milnshaw Park, and the purchase of the former Victoria Gardens was the first attempt by the Corporation to secure land for the purposes of a park. Oak Hill Park was opened in 1890, and in 1922 the war memorial was erected on land specially purchased by the Corporation to extend the park. Peel Park and parts of The Coppice originally belonged to William Peel of Knowlmere. The owner gave 35 acres, and the other 57 acres were purchased by the Corporation; the park opened in 1909. In September 1913, Tom Bullough gave the town 46 acres at Spring Hill in memory of his grandfather, and this came to be known as Bullough Park. Howard & Bullough presented the tennis courts in 1926. The house and grounds known as Hollins Hill, along with an endowment of £28,000, were bequeathed to the town in 1920 on the death of Anne Haworth, and Haworth Park opened in September 1921.

Milnshaw Park 1897 40124

Milnshaw Park was the first public park in Accrington, and was opened by Mayor John Emmanuel Lightfoot in July 1880. The Corporation had purchased what had been known as Victoria Gardens, and £2,000 was spent on laying out the grounds. Originally the park had an open-air swimming pool. This was filled in during the 1930s and made into a children's paddling pool.

Oak Hill Park 1899 43507

Oak Hill Park was Accrington's second park, and the land was purchased by the Corporation from Reginald Hargreaves for £12,000 in 1892. Work began in July of that year to prepare the estate for its opening as a park. The official opening took place on Whit Monday, 22 May 1893. It was an impressive occasion, as aldermen and councillors, and magistrates and mayors from the neighbouring towns joined the procession from the Town Hall. After the Mayor's speech of welcome, Reginald Hargreaves unlocked the main gates and the assembled crowds flooded into the park. The procession then moved to the bandstand, which had been presented by Councillor Joseph Duxbury; he had also given the new entrance gates and pillars. The Town Clerk, Mr Aitken, had provided swans and waterfowl to stock the lake which had been created, and the Accrington Brick and Tile Company had donated several terra-cotta vases which had been placed in various spots in the park.

The Rock Gardens, Oak Hill Park
c1955 A19010

The rock gardens were given in 1932 by Henry Parkinson, a founder member of Accrington Historical Association, in memory of his grandfather, also named Henry Parkinson. One of the stones was designated the 'wishing stone'.

▼ *The Rock Gardens, Oak Hill Park 2004* A19715

Rustic shelters and a bridge were added in 1933, along with inscribed granite boulders from Shap Fell.

▶ *The Rock Gardens, Oak Hill Park c1955* A19011

Japanese plants and shrubs were planted, and at the time it was said that Oak Hill Park had one of the finest rock gardens anywhere in the country. Slides of the rockery were shown at the Parks' Superintendents Conference at Swansea.

Inscribed Stone, the Rock Gardens, Oak Hill Park 2004 A19716

Here we see one of the inscribed stones, restored for the centenary of the park in 1993. It reads:

'There's not a tint that paints the rose

Or decks the lily fair

Or streaks the humblest flower that blows

But God has placed it there'.

Oak Hill Park 1897 40126

The drinking fountain, which still survives, was presented to the park by Alderman William Smith, the third Mayor of Accrington. The view shows the main entrance gates, presented by the late Councillor Joseph Duxbury.

Oak Hill Park 1897
40127

The original bandstand
was later converted
into an aviary. It was
replaced by a structure
which had started life
as a dais used on Peel
Street to receive their
Majesties King George V
and Queen Mary during
the royal visit of 1913.

► *Oak Hill Park c1935* A19001

This is the edge of the rock gardens, and we can see one of the terra-cotta vases (centre left). There were over two miles of footpaths in the park. The sign on the grass in the foreground reads 'No dogs allowed'.

◄ *Oak Hill Park c1935* A19008

Four cannons from the War Office were purchased by Henry Parkinson (calling himself 'Accrington Friend and Well Wisher'); two were sited on The Coppice, and two in Oak Hill Park. The guns were sent for war salvage in 1940.

▲ *Oak Hill Park 1897* 40128

At the time the park opened, Oak Hill Mansion was empty, having been tenanted from the time Jonathan Hargreaves left in 1856 until about 1880. It was said that the house, built in 1815, was second only in importance to Accrington House in its design and splendour.

◄ *The Museum, Oak Hill Park c1935* A19003

The Corporation renovated the house, and the museum opened in 1910. There were eight rooms displaying various eclectic items of local history, art and specialised collections. Most items were donated. During the Second World War, the museum closed to the public and never reopened. For some years in the 1950s and 1960s, Whitewell Dairies ran a café on the ground floor.

Oak Hill Mansion 2004 A19717

There was increasing concern over the state of the Mansion, which, despite being a listed building, was allowed to fall into dangerous disrepair. The misgivings of many were voiced in a public inquiry and the building was subsequently sold by the Council for £1.00, and the result has given new life to this attractive Georgian building. The extension erected by Jonathan Hargreaves was demolished at the time the Abbeyfield Society took over the house. It opened as a residential home for the elderly in 1995. Fortunately, many of the architectural features of the house have been retained.

The Haworth Art Gallery c1945 A19009

Hollins Hill was built in 1909 by William Haworth, as a home for himself and his sister Anne. The house was designed by the eminent architect, Walter Brierley of York (who also designed Dyke Nook, the home of the Blake family on Whalley Road). Built on the south side of the town in over 13 acres of park, Hollins Hill commanded a fine view of the hills. The formal rose garden was reputed to be one of the finest in Lancashire. The house imitates Tudor Architecture and the oak panelling and the oak staircase rank amongst the important features of the building. Carvings of flowers, animals and birds indicate William and Anne's love of nature.

In 1871 William Haworth had joined his father Thomas in the family cotton business; Thomas was a major employer and owned several mills. Twenty years later, William succeeded his father as head of the company, and expanded and improved the business.

Sadly, William died in 1913 so was not able to enjoy the pleasures of such a fine house for very long. After his death Anne, along with her companion and staff continued to live there. Anne died in 1920 and Hollins Hill was bequeathed to the Corporation of Accrington for use as an art gallery. In September 1921, the house, renamed the Haworth Art Gallery, opened as the town's first public art gallery.

In 1942 the gallery closed for the duration of the war and the pictures, together with several items from the museum at Clayton-le-Moors, were put into store. Contingency plans were made to utilise the gallery as an emergency hospital in case the Victoria Hospital was put out of action by enemy attacks and a system of fire watching was begun. Fortunately these plans came to nothing and the gallery began to be used as a hostel where off-duty service women, posted to this area, could spend their leisure time. The gallery reopened to the public in June 1945. Nowadays the gallery has achieved world-wide fame as the home of the largest collection of Tiffany glass in Europe.

51

CHURCHES
AND OTHER
MAJOR BUILDINGS

The massive growth in population and therefore building of all kinds peaked in 1911, having started in the early 1800s. This is reflected in the ecclesiastical and public buildings. Accrington was a chapelry of Altham and within Whalley parish. Despite being famous for its brick, Accrington is largely built of local stone, with many fine examples of the stonemason's art.

St James' Church c1945 A19007

Accrington was originally a chapelry of Altham. The chapel was built in 1763; it had no tower, and was considerably shorter. The chief benefactors of the church were the Peel and Hargreaves families, and Peel Street and Avenue Parade follow the route of the carriage drive from Accrington House, one of the homes of the Peels.

St James' Parish Church c1955 A19017

The trees soften the box-like lines of the church, and the well-filled graveyard contains many monuments to the people of Accrington. At the east end of the church the buildings of the Bay Horse Inn (demolished in 1959) can be seen.

St James' Church 2004 A19718

In 1967 Accrington Corporation took over the maintenance of the graveyard at St James' Church. Several tombstones were removed, and the graveyard was tidied.

▶ *St James' Church,*
Adam Westwell's Monument
2004 A19719

One interesting memorial is to Adam
Westwell, who played the ophicleide,
an instrument resembling a serpent.
It is sad that the sculpture of the
instrument itself is now missing.

▼ *St James' Church 1897* 40122

This view of the interior after its
reconstruction in 1880 shows the
delicate wrought iron work. All those
involved with building in this area
then would also be building the mills,
so it is therefore not surprising that
there are resemblances between
them. The view also illustrates the
relative importance of preaching over
the sacrament in those days: note the
extra height of the pulpit, which also
enabled the preacher to see and be
seen by those in the galleries.

▶ *The Accrington Pals*
Monument 2004 A19720

The new memorial was
unveiled on Sunday 4 July
2004; it commemorates the
granting of the Freedom of
the Borough of Hyndburn
to the Queen's Lancashire
Regiment. It is dedicated to
the East Lancashire Regiment
in memory of all ranks
who served and died in all
wars, particularly those of
the 11th Service Battalion
(Accrington), otherwise
known as the Accrington
Pals. The East Lancashire
Regiment, together with the
South Lancashire Regiment
and the Loyal Regiment
(North Lancashire), is the
forebear of the Queen's
Lancashire Regiment.
'Spectamur agendo' and
'Loyally I serve' are its
mottoes.

◀ *Christ Church 1897* 40120

Whilst some buildings in Accrington have remained virtually unchanged, others have been altered almost beyond recognition. Christ Church, built in 1840, is one such example. Severe dry rot, discovered in 1949, led to much heart-searching by church officials and the eventual decision to demolish the spire in 1954. In 1968 the roof was removed, and in March 1969 the church was re-hallowed following restoration.

Christ Church 2004
A19721

Without the finials and pinnacles it looks a much plainer building. Most of the memorials were removed at the restoration, but the windows are still retained, now protected against vandalism. The building is being put to multiple uses now as well as being a place of worship.

St John's Church 1899 43499

The Church of St John the Evangelist was completed in 1870. The new parish was carved out of St James' parish as more and more houses and industry were attracted to the Burnley Road area. It has always been the largest Church of England church in Accrington, accommodating 800 people before alterations in the last century. The tower, very much a feature of the townscape, is unusual in that it is constructed in three stages with freestanding pinnacles beside the spire.

St John's Church c1945 A19006

The interior view of St John's Church shows the east window depicting Christ holding the orb, flanked by St Peter and St Mary. It is a memorial to the Rev George Garbett, vicar of St James'. The wrought iron screen is particularly fine; it was erected in 1911 in memory of the Rev George Lomax, vicar for fifteen years. In 1992 the Accrington Pals Memorial Chapel was dedicated.

Sacred Heart Roman Catholic Church 1899 43503

Sacred Heart Roman Catholic Church was built during 1867 to accommodate the increasing number of Catholics in the area, and to replace St Oswald's Church on Hyndburn Road. The church was opened by Bishop Turner in August 1869. It was a matter of great sadness to many when the church was demolished in 2004.

The Roman Catholic Church, the Interior 1899 43504

The high altar was designed by Pugin and manufactured in Dublin at a cost of £700; it was of Gothic design and made of Caen stone, richly carved. It was given by James Lomax of Clayton Hall. Around the apse were figures of angels, and the church was rich in stained glass.

The New Jerusalem Church 1899 43500

Situated on Abbey Street next to the Swan Hotel, the New Jerusalem Church was one of the most striking buildings in the town. It was the largest Swedenborgian church in the country, and came to be known as the 'cathedral' of that denomination.

The New Jerusalem Church, the Interior 1899 43501

By 1983 the church was plagued by dry rot. The decision was made to demolish the building and in its place build a multi-purpose church, and the demolition of the church began in June 1987. The impressive organ was rescued and re-housed in a museum in Lincoln; the site of the church became a car park.

The New Church 2004 A19722

The two stained glass windows from the old church were installed in the new church on Hargreaves Street, which was dedicated in September 1985.

Cannon Street Baptist Church 1897 40123 (Photo from the collection at Accrington Library)

Cannon Street Baptist Church was built in 1873. Constructed of sandstone, this handsome church is a Grade II listed building. The spire is very much a feature of the townscape. In the early 1970s, the church was remodelled internally to create meeting rooms and worship areas. It is now troubled by dry rot and its future is uncertain.

61

▶ *The Cottage Hospital 1899* 43505

In January 1894, Accrington Corporation passed a resolution to establish a cottage hospital for Accrington and district. The design from the local architects was adopted, and the foundation stone was laid in 1895. The hospital was officially opened by the Mayor, Alderman Lee, in 1898, and named the Victoria Cottage Hospital in commemoration of the Queen's reign.

◀ *The Technical School 1899* 43498

The Technical School, designed by a local architect, Henry Ross, was erected by Accrington Corporation in 1895. It was officially opened on 28 August, with Henry Hills as its first headmaster. Both boys and girls were admitted, having first had to pass an entrance examination. Under the headmaster, Dr Edkins, the school was renamed Accrington Grammar School in 1921.

▲ *College Court 2004* A19723

Demolition of the Grammar School began in June 1998, and by the following January plans were approved for the building of these modern homes.

◄ *Greetings from Accrington, Composite c1965* A19035

The Rock Gardens at Oak Hill Park, Broadway with its new Arndale Centre, the bus station and St James' Church are all proudly portrayed here, with the Market Hall in the centre.

THE SURROUNDING TOWNSHIPS

The townships which now combine with Accrington to form the Borough of Hyndburn are Church, Clayton-le-Moors, Great Harwood, Oswaldtwistle, and Rishton, along with the parish of Altham. They have long had strong interconnections, but each retains its own fiercely protected identity.

ALTHAM, *The Church 1897* 40148

There has been a church at Altham since Norman times, and there may even have been a church there earlier. Altham was in a position of great importance to the De Lacy family, as it was on the route through to Clitheroe from Rossendale. Stones from the Norman church are preserved in the walls, and the font is Norman. The church was rebuilt in 1512, and major restorations were carried out in 1859, when the chancel was rebuilt and the tower and belfry were added.

BAXENDEN
The Church 1897 40129

The Church of St John the Baptist, Baxenden was completed in 1877 as the population in that area increased. Christ Church had opened in 1840, and Baxenden was originally part of that parish. The cost of the church was met by Miss Pilling-Taylor and her sister Mrs Edwards-Taylor of Moreton Hall.

CHURCH, *Church Kirk 1897* 40131

St James' Church Kirk is a place of worship of very ancient origin. 'Church' is a Northumbrian word and 'Kirk' is Mercian; both words mean 'a place of worship'. Coupling the two words together in this way is the only example of its kind in Britain, and the township around it adopted the name Church. It has been suggested that there must be strong reasons for the name, and the connections with St Oswald, the hero king of Northumbria, are the most likely. The tower of the church is early Perpendicular, and it was used as a watchtower by Rishton families during the Wars of the Roses. The nave was rebuilt in 1804, when an ancient mellow structure was exchanged for a more utilitarian design. The tower suffered a fire as recently as 1982, which caused internal damage, particularly to the bells and the clock. A redundant peal of bells was brought from Christ Church, Pendlebury to replace the damaged peal.

CLAYTON-LE-MOORS
Dunkenhalgh 1897
40140

The building is on the site of previous houses owned by the Rishton family; Dunkenhalgh then passed to the Walmsleys, until Catherine Walmsley married Robert the seventh Lord Petre. It continued in the Petre family, staunch Catholics, until 1939.

CLAYTON-LE-MOORS, *Dunkenhalgh Avenue 1897* 40141

Dunkenhalgh was sold in April 1947 when it was converted into a hotel. As part of the agreement, the magnificent drive and avenue of limes were to be preserved 'for ever and a day'.

CLAYTON-LE-MOORS, *All Saints' Church 1899* 43509

The church was designed by John Harper, the son of the Dunkenhalgh land agent, and was consecrated in October 1840 by the Bishop of Chester.

CLAYTON-LE-MOORS
All Saints' Church 1897
40133

Originally, St James', Altham had served the Clayton-le-Moors area, but the expanding population of Clayton led John Mercer, a devout Methodist, to realise the need for an Anglican church. He was the inventor of the mercerisation process, and was a self-taught chemist of great eminence. He persuaded John Fort, a partner at Oakenshaw Printworks, to give the site, and the printworks employees contributed generously to the building fund.

CLAYTON-LE-MOORS, *All Saints' Church, the Interior 1897* 40134

The church was originally a plain rectangular building with a tower, but by 1852 galleries were added to provide more seating and an organ was installed. The most spectacular change took place in 1882, when the chancel and east window were added.

CLAYTON-LE-MOORS, *All Saints' Church, the Interior 1897* 40136

The font, reredos and chancel furnishings were mostly of marble, gaining for All Saints' the reputation of being 'the marble church'.

CLAYTON-LE-MOORS,
*St Mary's Roman
Catholic Church 1899*
43510

St Mary's Roman Catholic
Church on Burnley Road,
Clayton-le-Moors dated
back to 1819, and predated
all other Roman Catholic
churches in the area.
The church was a plain
rectangular structure, of no
real architectural merit. The
new church on Devonshire
Drive was opened in
September 1959; the old
church was demolished in
the same year.

▲ CLAYTON-LE-MOORS
St Mary's Roman Catholic Church, the Interior 1899
43511

The plain exterior was compensated for by a lavishly decorated interior. The silver sanctuary lamp came from the chapel at Dunkenhalgh, and so did the silver thurible and a large crucifix. The picture over the altar represented the presentation of Christ in the temple, and was considered to be a rare and costly work of art.

► *detail from 43511*

▲ **CLAYTON-LE-MOORS**
*The Wesleyan Chapel, the Interior
1899* 43513

In 1867 the gallery was added. The front of
the church was altered in 1913 to provide
a porch, and the church was described
as being the most beautiful and best
equipped in the neighbourhood. The
church was demolished in 1981, and the
congregation moved into the Sunday
School.

◀ *detail from 43513*

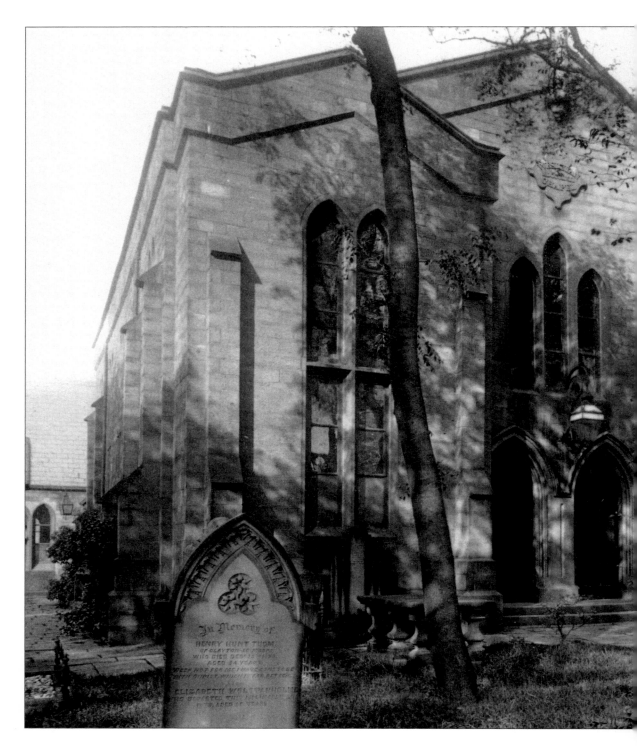

CLAYTON-LE-MOORS
*The Wesleyan Chapel
1897* 40137

Barnes Square Methodist Church was built in 1863, replacing an earlier building which had become too small. John Mercer laid the foundation stone.

GREAT HARWOOD
The Church 1897 40142

Great Harwood has always been an isolated community. It has been bypassed by all major routes, whether road, rail or canal, and is situated in a most beautiful spot. The earliest mention of the chapel of Great Harwood is in a deed of 1335. The church nestles halfway up the hill, surrounded by trees, and facing outwards to the town. It was built as a Chapel of Ease to Blackburn. The tower dates from the 15th century and the nave from the 16th century; the church remained unaltered until 1881, when it was decided to lengthen it and build a new chancel. At some point, the dedication was changed from St Lawrence to St Bartholomew; the original dedication is commemorated in St Lawrence Street. One famous son of Great Harwood, John Mercer, is buried in the churchyard.

GREAT HARWOOD
The Roman Catholic Church 1898 40143

The Church of Our Lady and St Hubert, Great Harwood was consecrated in 1859. It was founded by James Lomax of Clayton Hall, who gave £6000 to the building fund and also endowed it with other money. It was designed in the Gothic Revival tradition by Welby Pugin. James Lomax was buried in the family tomb under the altar of the Lady Chapel.

GREAT HARWOOD, *Cock Bridge 1897* 40146

Cock Bridge takes Whalley Road across the River Calder (now much cleaner than it used to be) and links Great Harwood and Whalley. This stone bridge is in an attractive spot, popular with walkers, as many good footpaths from Great Harwood, Whalley and Read converge here. Just above the bridge on the Great Harwood side is the Game Cock Inn.

STANHILL
Stanhill Lane
c1955 S814004

STANHILL, *Stanhill Lane c1955* S814005

This road is lined by the attractive semi-detached Russell-built houses of the 1930s. At one time, Stanhill was an isolated hamlet on the road between Blackburn and Oswaldtwistle, and it is most famous as being the home of the inventor James Hargreaves.

STANHILL
*Robert Peel's
Homestead
c1955* S814001

STANHILL, *Robert Peel's Homestead c1955* S814002

Peel Fold, situated on the slope of a hill a short distance away from the main road, was originally known as Oldham's Cross. Robert Peele, great-grandfather of the first baronet, purchased the property towards the end of the 17th century. The great residences which the Peels built in Hyndburn have been swept away, but this Tudor cottage, now lovingly restored, remains as a monument to one of Lancashire's great families.

STANHILL
The Post Office
c1955 S814003

STANHILL, *The Post Office, James Hargreaves Cottage c1955* S814008

Stanhill Post Office was the home of James Hargreaves, the inventor in 1764 of the Spinning Jenny. His invention made an enormous contribution to the textile industry. He was born in Stanhill in 1720 and married and settled there; he became a handloom weaver.

STANHILL
The James Hargreaves Memorial Garden
c1955 S814007

James Hargreaves was connected with Robert Peel through helping him to introduce mechanical processes at Brookside Mill, so it was appropriate that the James Hargreaves memorial should be unveiled in July 1952 by Earl Peel of Hyning Hall, Carnforth. The inscribed plaque on the cottage told the story of how Hargreaves was compelled to leave Stanhill because of persecution by local handloom weavers who feared for their livelihoods. Hargreaves moved to Nottingham, and died there in comparative obscurity in April 1778.

WHALLEY, *Moreton Hall 1897* 40144

Moreton Hall, Whalley lies just over the boundary from Great
Harwood at the other side of the valley of the Calder. The original
house was built about 1490, and remained in the Moreton family
for many years. Later it was home to the Nowells and then the
Taylors. It was built after designs by George Webster of Kendal,
and was reputed to be a 'calendar' house, with the number of
features corresponding to the days and months of the year. It was
demolished in the 1950s after wartime occupation by the army
and later by the Polish Resettlement Unit.

INDEX

FRITH PRODUCTS & SERVICES

Francis Frith would doubtless be pleased to know that the pioneering publishing venture he started in 1860 still continues today. Over a hundred and forty years later, The Francis Frith Collection continues in the same innovative tradition and is now one of the foremost publishers of vintage photographs in the world. Some of the current activities include:

INTERIOR DECORATION

Today Frith's photographs can be seen framed and as giant wall murals in thousands of pubs, restaurants, hotels, banks, retail stores and other public buildings throughout the country. In every case they enhance the unique local atmosphere of the places they depict and provide reminders of gentler days in an increasingly busy and frenetic world.

PRODUCT PROMOTIONS

Frith products are used by many major companies to promote the sales of their own products or to reinforce their own history and heritage. Frith promotions have been used by Hovis bread, Courage beers, Scots Porage Oats, Colman's mustard, Cadbury's foods, Mellow Birds coffee, Dunhill pipe tobacco, Guinness, and Bulmer's Cider.

GENEALOGY AND FAMILY HISTORY

As the interest in family history and roots grows world-wide, more and more people are turning to Frith's photographs of Great Britain for images of the towns, villages and streets where their ancestors lived; and, of course, photographs of the churches and chapels where their ancestors were christened, married and buried are an essential part of every genealogy tree and family album.

FRITH PRODUCTS

All Frith photographs are available Framed or just as Mounted Prints and unmounted versions. These may be ordered from the address below. Other products available are - Calendars, Jigsaws, Canvas Prints, Mugs, Tea Towels, Tableware and local and prestige books.

THE INTERNET

Over several hundred thousand Frith photographs can be viewed and purchased on the internet through the Frith websites!

For more detailed information on Frith products, look at
www.francisfrith.com

See the complete list of Frith Books at: www.francisfrith.com
This web site is regularly updated with the latest list of publications from The Francis Frith Collection. If you wish to buy books relating to another part of the country that your local bookshop does not stock, you may purchase on-line.

For further information, trade, or author enquiries please contact us at the address below:
The Francis Frith Collection, Unit 19 Kingsmead Business Park, Gillingham, Dorset SP8 5FB.
Tel: +44 (0)1722 716 376   Email: sales@francisfrith.co.uk

See Frith products on the internet at www.francisfrith.com

FREE PRINT OF YOUR CHOICE
CHOOSE A PHOTOGRAPH FROM THIS BOOK

+ POSTAGE

Mounted Print
Overall size 14 x 11 inches (355 x 280mm)

TO RECEIVE YOUR FREE PRINT

Choose any Frith photograph in this book

Simply complete the Voucher opposite and return it with your payment (to cover postage and handling) and we will print the photograph of your choice in SEPIA (size 11 x 8 inches) and supply it in a cream mount ready to frame (overall size 14 x 11 inches).

Order additional Mounted Prints
at HALF PRICE - £19.00 each (normally £38.00)

If you would like to order more Frith prints from this book, possibly as gifts for friends and family, you can buy them at half price (with no additional postage costs).

Have your Mounted Prints framed

For an extra £20.00 per print you can have your mounted print(s) framed in an elegant polished wood and gilt moulding, overall size 16 x 13 inches (no additional postage required).

IMPORTANT!

❶ Please note: aerial photographs and photographs with a reference number starting with a "Z" are not Frith photographs and cannot be supplied under this offer.

❷ Offer valid for delivery to one UK address only.

❸ These special prices are only available if you use this form to order. You must use the ORIGINAL VOUCHER on this page (no copies permitted). We can only despatch to one UK address.

❹ This offer cannot be combined with any other offer.

As a customer your name & address will be stored by Frith but not sold or rented to third parties. Your data will be used for the purpose of this promotion only.

Send completed Voucher form to:
The Francis Frith Collection,
19 Kingsmead Business Park, Gillingham,
Dorset SP8 5FB

Voucher for **FREE** and Reduced Price Frith Prints

Please do not photocopy this voucher. Only the original is valid, so please fill it in, cut it out and return it to us with your order.

Picture ref no	Page no	Qty	Mounted @ £19.00	Framed + £20.00	Total Cost £
		1	Free of charge*	£	£
			£19.00	£	£
			£19.00	£	£
			£19.00	£	£
			£19.00	£	£
			£19.00	£	£
Please allow 28 days for delivery. Offer available to one UK address only			* Post & handling		£3.80
			Total Order Cost		£

Title of this book . . . .

I enclose a cheque/postal order for £ . . . . made payable to 'The Francis Frith Collection'

OR please debit my Mastercard / Visa / Maestro card, details below

Card Number:

Issue No (Maestro only):   Valid from (Maestro):

Card Security Number: Expires:

Signature:

Name Mr/Mrs/Ms . . . .

Address . . . .

. . . .

. . . .

. . . . Postcode . . . .

Daytime Tel No . . . .

Email . . . .

Valid to 31/12/20

Can you help us with information about any of the Frith photographs in this book?

We are gradually compiling an historical record for each of the photographs in the Frith archive. It is always fascinating to find out the names of the people shown in the pictures, as well as insights into the shops, buildings and other features depicted.

If you recognize anyone in the photographs in this book, or if you have information not already included in the author's caption, do let us know. We would love to hear from you, and will try to publish it in future books or articles.

An Invitation from The Francis Frith Collection to Share Your Memories

The 'Share Your Memories' feature of our website allows members of the public to add personal memories relating to the places featured in our photographs, or comment on others already added. Seeing a place from your past can rekindle forgotten or long held memories. Why not visit the website, find photographs of places you know well and add YOUR story for others to read and enjoy? We would love to hear from you!

www.francisfrith.com/memories

Our production team

Frith books are produced by a small dedicated team at offices near Salisbury. Most have worked with the Frith Collection for many years. All have in common one quality: they have a passion for the Frith Collection.

Frith Books and Gifts

We have a wide range of books and gifts available on our website utilising our photographic archive, many of which can be individually personalised.

www.francisfrith.com